ANIMALS

Baboons

by Kevin J. Holmes

Consultant:
Dr. Debra L. Forthman
Director of Field Conservation
Zoo Atlanta

Bridgestone Books
an imprint of Capstone Press
Mankato, Minnesota

Bridgestone Books are published by Capstone Press
151 Good Counsel Drive, P.O. Box 669, Mankato, Minnesota 56002
http://www.capstone-press.com

Library of Congress Cataloging-in-Publication Data
Holmes, Kevin J.
    Baboons/by Kevin J. Holmes.
        p. cm.—(Animals)
    Includes bibliographical references (p. 23) and index.
    Summary: Introduces the baboon's physical characteristics, habits, food, and
relationship to humans.
    ISBN 0-7368-0494-3
    1. Baboons—Juvenile literature. [1. Baboons] I. Title. II. Animals (Mankato, Minn.)
QL737.P93 H66 2000
599.8'65—dc21

                                                                    99-054147

Editorial Credits
Erika Mikkelson, editor; Timothy Halldin, cover designer; Kimberly Danger, photo
    researcher

Photo Credits
Gerald D. Tang, 20
Joe McDonald, 8, 14
Leonard Rue Enterprises, cover, 4, 16
Rob and Ann Simpson, 10, 12
Robin Brandt, 6
Unicorn Stock Photos/Rod Furgason, 18

1 2 3 4 5 6 05 04 03 02 01 00

Table of Contents

Eyes

Tail

Mouth

Legs

Fast Facts

Family: Baboons belong to the *Cercopithecidae* family. A family is a group of animals with similar features.

Range: Baboons live in Africa.

Habitat: Baboons live in forests, on savannas, or on rocky hills. Baboons eat the grass and plants that grow on the flat savannas.

Food: Baboons also eat fruits, nuts, and seeds. They sometimes eat rabbits, lizards, grasshoppers, and other small animals.

Mating: Baboons mate year-round to produce young. Female baboons start to mate when they are 5 years old. Male baboons start to mate when they are 7 years old.

Young: Young baboons drink their mothers' milk until they are 6 to 8 months old. Young baboons are called infants.

Baboons

Baboons are primates. Primates are a group of animals that includes humans, apes, and monkeys. Primates have thumbs. This feature makes them different from other animals. Baboons are a kind of large monkey.

Baboons and other primates are mammals. Mammals are warm-blooded animals that have a backbone. The body heat of warm-blooded animals does not change with the weather. Female mammals feed milk to their young.

Six kinds of baboons exist in the world. Olive baboons, chacma baboons, yellow baboons, and brown baboons live on the African savannas. The savanna baboons are the most common. The hamadryas baboons and the gelada baboons live in the deserts of northeastern Africa.

The olive baboon is one of the six kinds of baboons.

Appearance

Baboons are the largest of all monkeys. They weigh 26 to 90 pounds (12 to 41 kilograms).

A baboon can be one of many colors. Baboons with brown or gray hair are the most common. But some baboons are more colorful. Gelada baboons have pink chests. The pink area is the baboon's skin. Gray and white hair grows around the pink area. Geladas sometimes are called "bleeding heart baboons" because of their pink chests.

Baboons often are called "dog-faced" monkeys. Their jaws stick out like the jaw of a dog. Baboons also have very sharp, doglike teeth. Baboons yawn and show their teeth to warn possible attackers.

Baboons show their teeth to scare away attackers.

Homes

Baboons live in Africa. They make their homes in a variety of habitats. Most baboons live in forests or on savannas. Both habitats have many of the foods baboons eat.

Some baboons live in national parks or reserves in Africa. Baboons in these protected areas have plenty of space to roam.

Gelada baboons live in the mountains of northeastern Africa. Hamadryas baboons often are found in the open, rocky hill country of this area.

Baboons spend most of their time on the ground. But they are excellent climbers. Baboons climb trees to feed on fruits, flowers, and seeds. They also climb trees when it is time to sleep. Baboons hide in trees if they are in danger.

Baboons climb trees to escape attackers and to find food.

Mating and Young

Male and female baboons mate to produce young. Female baboons begin mating when they are about 5 years old. Most male baboons start mating when they are 7 years old. Baboon mothers usually give birth to one infant at a time.

Young baboons often ride on their mothers when a group travels. The young baboons are not strong enough to keep up with the other baboons. Newborn baboons cling to their mothers' stomachs. Older baboons ride on their mothers' backs. Young baboons must hold on tight. If the young baboons fall off, they could be hurt or eaten by enemies.

A baboon's childhood lasts about three years. During this time, baboons play with other young baboons. They learn how to live in a group. Female baboons stay with their mothers for life. Males leave their birth group when they are between 4 and 6 years old. Alone or with another male, they search for another group to join.

A young baboon hangs on to its mother while she runs.

13

Troops

Most baboons live in groups called troops. Some troops have as many as 200 members. Other baboons travel in smaller troops. Gelada and hamadryas baboons usually have one male, several females, and their young in a troop.

Members of a troop are very close to each other. They groom each other every day. They clean each other's hair with their fingers, tongues, and teeth. They pick out dirt, insects, and dry skin. Grooming helps to create close ties between baboons. Baboons relax when they groom each other.

Each baboon troop has a social order. The most experienced males and females are in charge of the troop. Each baboon has its own place in the troop.

Young baboons quickly learn their place. If they cause trouble, the older baboons will punish them. Young males that enter the troop sometimes will try to take control. When this happens, male baboons may fight for control of the troop.

Baboons usually groom each other before and after eating.

Food

Baboons are omnivores. Omnivorous animals eat both plants and animals. Most baboons eat fruits, nuts, and grasses. They eat rabbits, lizards, and grasshoppers. Baboons also may kill and eat young antelope and birds.

Baboons usually walk about 5 miles (8 kilometers) each day in search of food and water. They must stop at least once a day to drink water. Baboons dig for water during the dry season. They dig holes in dry riverbeds to find water.

Baboons must be careful when drinking from a river or watering hole. Crocodiles and other enemies may hide in or near the water. Enemies will attack baboons that are not careful. Baboons that are alone are easy targets for leopards and other enemies.

A chacma baboon watches for crocodiles while it drinks.

Predators

Baboons have many predators. Predators hunt and kill other animals. Lions, leopards, crocodiles, and wild dogs try to kill baboons.

Traveling in troops protects the baboons from attackers. The females and the young travel at the center of the troop. The strongest males travel next to the females. The rest of the male baboons travel at the outer edges of the troop. These baboons look for predators. If a predator moves too close, the outer male baboons rush out to meet it. The strongest males protect the females and the young.

Baboons are difficult to attack because of their size and the way they travel. Predators usually attack sick baboons or baboons that have wandered away from the troop. Groups of adult male baboons are too large and dangerous to attack. Baboons warn other baboons when a predator is near by using loud, barking calls.

Baboons work together to protect their troop from predators.